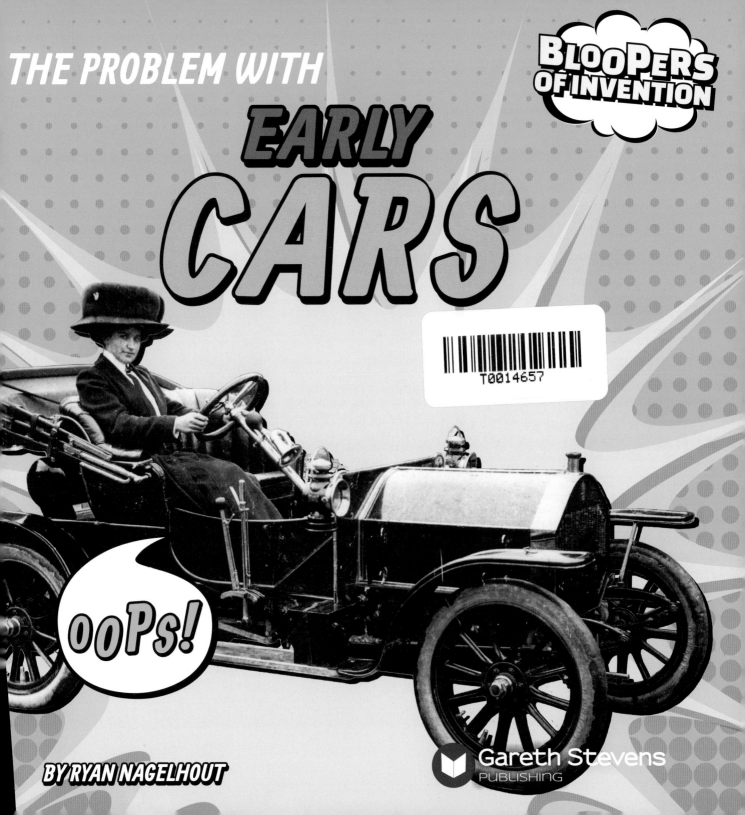

Please visit our website, www.garethstevens.com. For a free color catalog of all our high-quality books, call toll free 1-800-542-2595 or fax 1-877-542-2596.

Library of Congress Cataloging-in-Publication Data

Nagelhout, Ryan.
The problem with early cars / by Ryan Nagelhout.
p. cm. — (Bloopers of invention)
Includes index.
ISBN 978-1-4824-2760-8 (pbk.)
ISBN 978-1-4824-2761-5 (6 pack)
ISBN 978-1-4824-2762-2 (library binding)
1. Automobiles — Juvenile literature. 2. Automobiles — History — Juvenile literature. I. Nagelhout, Ryan.
II. Title.
TL147.N34 2016
629.222—d23

First Edition

Published in 2016 by
Gareth Stevens Publishing
111 East 14th Street, Suite 349
New York, NY 10003

Copyright © 2016 Gareth Stevens Publishing

Designer: Sarah Liddell
Editor: Ryan Nagelhout

Photo credits: Cover, p. 1 Heritage Images/Contributor/Hulton Archive/Getty Images; p. 5 Superstock/ Getty Images; p. 7 (photo) Science & Society Picture Library/Contributor/SSPL/Getty Images; p. 7 (diagram) Stahlkocher/Wikimedia Commons; pp. 9 (main), 19 (Dymaxion) Car Culture/Car Culture ® Collection/Getty Images; p. 9 (taxi) BArchBot/Wikimedia Commons; p. 11 (main) De Agostini Picture Library/Getty Images; p. 11 (Karl Benz) 83d40m/Wikimedia Commons; p. 13 (main) Fox Photos/Stringer/Hulton Archive/Getty Images; p. 13 (inset) Hulton Collection/Hulton Archive/ Getty Images; p. 15 (main) MPI/Stronger/Archive Photos/Getty Images; p. 15 (Ford) Scewing/ Wikimedia Commons; p. 17 (main) Hulton Archive/Stringer/Getty Images; p. 17 (model T truck) James K. Troxell/Shutterstock.com; p. 19 (Buckminster Fuller) Bachrach/Contributor/Getty Images; p. 21 (main) Robert King/Staff/Hulton Archive/Getty Images; p. 21 (Chevy Corvair) The Enthusiast Network/Contributor/Getty Images.

All rights reserved. No part of this book may be reproduced in any form without permission in writing from the publisher, except by a reviewer.

Printed in the United States of America

CPSIA compliance information: Batch #CS15GS: For further information contact Gareth Stevens, New York, New York at 1-800-542-2595.

CONTENTS

Words in the glossary appear in **bold** type the first time they are used in the text.

THE HORSELESS CARRIAGE

Can you imagine a world without cars? You might not be able to, but the history of the automobile is fairly brief. The "horseless **carriage**" was a new invention in the 19th century. Before that, people could only get somewhere as fast as a horse could take them.

Making the first cars was hard, and lots of mistakes were made. The **vehicles** broke down, and they couldn't go very fast. They were nothing like the safe, dependable cars we have today!

OOPs!

Italian inventors had ideas for wind-driven vehicles as far back as the 14th century!

MODERN AUTOMOBILES ARE ALSO CALLED MOTOR VEHICLES. THERE ARE MANY DIFFERENT KINDS, SUCH AS CARS, TRUCKS, AND SUVs.

5

STEAM MACHINES

Many early vehicles were powered by steam. Steam engines work by heating water to make it a gas, then **compressing** the gas and using its power to create movement.

French inventor Nicolas-Joseph Cugnot made the first steam-powered automobile in 1769. The vehicle was a three-wheeled tractor he made for the French army. It moved just 2.25 miles (3.6 km) per hour! Early steam-powered cars were too heavy to drive on dirt roads. Iron rails had to be put down to keep them from getting stuck.

OOPs!

In 1834, a steam carriage built by John Scott Russell exploded! Four people died in the accident, and Russell went out of business.

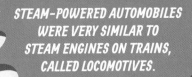

STEAM-POWERED AUTOMOBILES WERE VERY SIMILAR TO STEAM ENGINES ON TRAINS, CALLED LOCOMOTIVES.

THE CUGNOT STEAMER

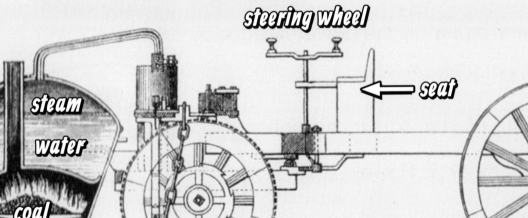

steering wheel

seat

steam

water

coal

boiler

front wheel

two back wheels

ELECTRIC CARS

At the start of the 20th century, almost 35 percent of automobiles were powered by electricity. Electric cars had some advantages over gas or steam cars. Early gas cars were loud and shook while they were running. Electric cars were quiet and had big **batteries** in them to supply the power needed to drive.

More than 20 companies were making electric cars in the United States by 1912. However, the slow charging time of batteries and limited driving range made them less popular over time.

OOPs!

Early electric cars could only move 15–20 miles (24–32 km) per hour and travel 30–40 miles (48–64 km) per charge.

THERE WERE NOT MANY PLACES WITH ELECTRICITY TO CHARGE CAR BATTERIES IN THE EARLY 20TH CENTURY.

electric taxi cab

9

BENZ'S AUTOMOBILE

One problem with early cars was trying to find a fuel that would work with an internal **combustion** engine. German inventor Karl Benz is credited with creating the first true automobile in 1885. The car ran on gasoline, which most cars still use today.

Benz's first car was a three-wheeled machine with a one-**cylinder** gasoline engine. A spark inside the engine lit the gas on fire, forcing a **piston** inside to move. The movement inside the engine pushed the car forward.

OOPS!

Benz made four laps around a small track on his first ride, *stalling* twice before a broken chain stopped the car for good.

BENZ'S FIRST SALE CAME IN 1888 TO A PARISIAN MAN NAMED ÉMILE ROGER.

Karl Benz

MISSING PARTS

Early cars also lacked many of the features we enjoy in cars today. Most didn't have roofs, windshields, or lights to drive at night. They could only fit two people in them, and there were no airbags or other safety equipment.

That's because most cars didn't go very fast at first. But just 15 years after the first electric "horseless carriage" was introduced in Chicago in 1893, cars were going 60 miles (97 km) per hour!

OOPS!

The first person officially considered to die in a "true" car accident was Mary Ward, a scientist who was thrown from a steam car in 1869.

FORD'S QUADRICYCLE

American inventor Henry Ford and some friends made a vehicle called the Quadricycle in 1896. It had a gas engine and four large bicycle wheels to ride on. The Quadricycle was steered by a rudder, like a boat. The small car only had two gears and couldn't move backward.

Ford was the first to drive it, going a few blocks down the road before it broke down. Ford soon started his own car company and started working on a better model.

OOPS!

Ford built his Quadricycle in a brick shed. When it was ready to drive, he had to knock down a wall with an ax because it didn't fit through the door!

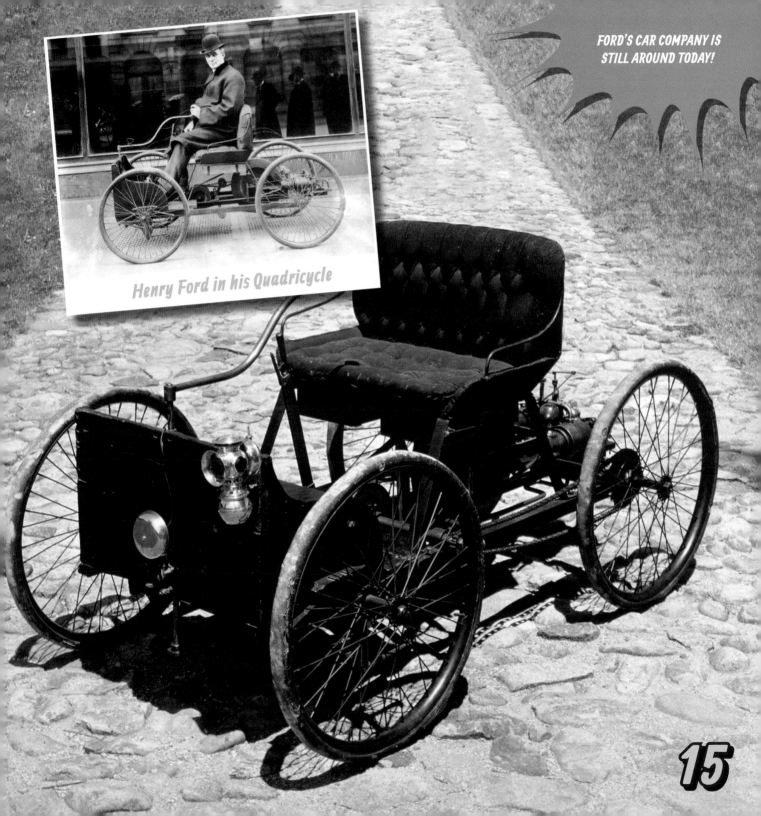

Henry Ford in his Quadricycle

THE MODEL T

Ford's most important car, the Model T, changed the world. Introduced in 1908, the Model T cost $825. It was a simple car that was easy for people to use. But it was far from the perfect car. It only came in black and was started with a hand crank.

OOPS!

The Model T used gravity to bring gas to its engine. It was also more powerful in reverse, which meant it often had to be driven up steep hills backward!

Many early cars got stuck on muddy roads easily. Most places didn't have **paved** roads at all, which could also make driving hard.

Ford Model T truck

THREE WHEELS?

Three-wheeled cars were all the rage in the early days of automobiles. Why aren't there any on the roads today? Well, many people simply thought four wheels were better than three! Three-wheel cars can also be hard to steer and have balance issues.

American inventor Richard Buckminster Fuller designed one three-wheeler, the Dymaxion, in 1933. Two people died during testing, and an accident at the 1933 World's Fair in Chicago helped make sure the car was never sold.

OOPS!

A few people put in orders for their own Dymaxion, including the famous *aviator* Amelia Earhart. The car was never put into full production. Only three were ever made!

Richard Buckminster Fuller

DYMAXION

MODERN MISHAPS

Today's cars are safer and more reliable, but they can still be dangerous. Different parts can be **recalled** if drivers could get hurt because the car won't work properly. In 2014, General Motors recalled a whopping 28 million cars around the world for a number of different reasons.

Tires can also be a problem on modern cars. In 2001, a recall of Firestone tires on Ford Explorer SUVs ended a 100-year relationship between the two companies. No matter how advanced cars become, there will probably always be bloopers!

OOPS!
Ralph Nader's 1965 book Unsafe at Any Speed called the Chevy Corvair "The One-Car Accident." The book also helped force many states to pass seat belt and other safety laws.

Chevy Corvair

GLOSSARY

aviator: a pilot, or someone who flies airplanes

battery: a device that turns chemical energy into electricity

carriage: a horse-drawn wheeled wagon made to carry people

combustion: an act or instance of burning

compress: to squeeze together

cylinder: a tube-shaped space in a gasoline engine in which a piston moves up and down to create power

environment: the conditions that surround a living thing and affect the way it lives

paved: covered with hard matter to make a road

piston: a piece in an engine that slides up and down in the cylinder as it makes power for the engine

recall: to call back

stall: to delay or pause

vehicle: an object that moves people from place to place

FOR MORE INFORMATION

BOOKS

Baxter, Roberta. *The First Cars.* Mankato, MN: Capstone Press, 2015.

Fawcett, Bill. *It Looked Good on Paper: Bizarre Inventions, Design Disasters, and Engineering Follies.* New York, NY: Harper, 2009.

Lassieur, Allison. *Cars 100 Years Ago.* Mankato, MN: Amicus, 2012.

WEBSITES

Model T
history.com/topics/model-t
Find out more about Henry Ford's Model T.

Who Invented the Automobile?
loc.gov/rr/scitech/mysteries/auto.html
Find out more about Karl Benz and his first automobile on this site.

Publisher's note to educators and parents: Our editors have carefully reviewed these websites to ensure that they are suitable for students. Many websites change frequently, however, and we cannot guarantee that a site's future contents will continue to meet our high standards of quality and educational value. Be advised that students should be closely supervised whenever they access the Internet.

INDEX